Bear Story

By Joy Martin – Illustrated by Shannon Cartwright

Bear Story: A Rhyme from A to Zzzz's

11 10 9 8 7

Martin, Joy
Bear Story: A Rhyme from A to Zzzz's written by Joy Martin; illustrated by Shannon Cartwright.
(1. Bears—Fiction. 2. Stories in rhyme.) 1. Title: *Bear Story: A rhyme from A to Zzzz's*.
II. Cartwright, Shannon, ill. III. Title.

ISBN 978-1-940381-13-8

Published by:
Greatland Graphics
3875 Geist Rd, Ste E PMB 449
Fairbanks, Alaska 99709
GreatlandGraphics.com
Printed in Canada

Aa Bb Cc Dd Ee Ff Gg Hh Ii Jj Kk Ll Mm
Nn Oo Pp Qq Rr Ss Tt Uu Vv Ww Xx Yy Zz

Inspired by wide-awake Rustin Crandall
who "toddlered" off to sweet dreams with
loving versions of Bear Story.
—J. M.

Dedicated to my wonderful mother
and bears everywhere.
— S. C.

Aa Bb Cc Dd Ee Ff Gg Hh Ii Jj Kk Ll Mm
Nn Oo Pp Qq Rr Ss Tt Uu Vv Ww Xx Yy Zz

A a

A bright spring breaks
through melting snows.

A a   A bright spring breaks through melting snows.

B b

Baby bears yawn
and touch mom's nose.

B b   Baby bears yawn and touch mom's nose.

Cc

Cubs and mother
peek-a-boo out.

C c Cubs and mother peek-a-boo out.

D d

Down slopes they slide
on rump and snout.

D d   Down slopes they slide on rump and snout.

E e

Each blade of grass smells sweet and new.

E e   Each blade of grass smells sweet and new.

F f

Feeding bears sniff,
nibble and chew.

F f   Feeding bears sniff, nibble and chew.

G g

Growing cubs hunt
and play for hours.

G g   Growing cubs hunt and play for hours.

H h

Hills of bright green burst with flowers.

H h   Hills of bright green burst with flowers.

I i

In summer's warmth,
creeks gurgle clear.

I i   In summer's warmth, creeks gurgle clear.

J j

Jolly cubs fish
while mom rests near.

Jj   Jolly cubs fish while mom rests near.

K k

Keeping back now,
they watch mom climb.

K k Keeping back now, they watch mom climb.

L l

Little bears try,
falling each time.

L l   Little bears try, falling each time.

M m

Mother bear basks in autumn sun.

M m   Mother bear basks in autumn sun.

N n   Naughty twins pounce on her in fun.

N n   Naughty twins pounce on her in fun.

O o

Overhead, geese
start their long flights south.

O o   Overhead, geese start their long flights south.

P p

Pudgy cub stoops to fill his mouth.

P p   Pudgy cub stoops to fill his mouth.

Q q

Quickly mom feels winter's first chill.

2 q   Quickly mom feels winter's first chill.

R r

Rousting both cubs,
she leads up hill.

R r   Rousting both cubs, she leads up hill.

S s

Sleepy bears seek a safe, warm den.

S s   Sleepy bears seek a safe, warm den.

T t

Threatening winds whoosh.
Leaves fall. Trees bend.

T t Threatening winds whoosh. Leaves fall. Trees bend.

U u

Under her arms,
cubs cuddle tight.

U u   Under her arms, cubs cuddle tight.

V v

Vocal owls hoot
throughout the night.

V v   Vocal owls hoot throughout the night.

Ww

Winter rest slows
the bears' heartbeat.

W w Winter rest slows the bears' heartbeat.

X x

X marks the spot
of their retreat.

X x   X marks the spot of their retreat.

Y y

Z Z Z Z Z Z Z

Yawning, snoring, the three bears sleep.

Y y Yawning, snoring, the three bears sleep.

Z z

Zzzz's echo through
the snow so deep.

Z z   Zzzz's echo through the snow so deep.

Facts about bears

Ursus arctos

Grizzly and brown bears were once considered separate species; people still describe the larger coastal bears as brown bears and the relatively smaller interior bears as grizzlies. The male bear is called a boar, the female is called a sow, and the young are called cubs. Brown bears have excellent hearing and a superior sense of smell. Their eyesight is good.

Cubs

Brown bears mate between May and July. Cubs are born in their den between January and March; litters range from one to four, but two is the most common. Cubs weigh less than a pound at birth and are born hairless and blind. They gain weight quickly and rely heavily on their mother's milk during their first months of life. A first-year cub may weigh 100 pounds by October. Cubs usually leave their mothers at the start of their third summer.

Food

Brown bears are omnivorous, eating various foods such as grasses, berries, honey, fish, roots, insects, nuts, and game, and scavenged meat such as beached whales. Bears are sloppy eaters and drool a lot. They are very powerful and can dig 100 pounds of dirt while seeking roots or rodents in tunnels. Bears can run 30 miles per hour.

Sounds

Bears make lots of sounds. They whine, grumble, yawn, woof, coo, and grunt. When startled or angered, they make warning coughs and will pop teeth and chomp jaws. The cubs will bawl if scared.

Sleep

Since food is scarce in winter, bears hibernate. Their body temperature drops slightly, their heartbeat slows, and they don't eat, drink, urinate or defecate. They breathe four to five times per minute in "winter rest." They may remain in their den for up to six months, but there are reports of some bears being active all winter in areas where food is available. The dens may have openings under trees or ledges that create overhangs.

Range/Habitat
Brown bears are found throughout most of Alaska except the far Aleutian Islands. Alaska is home to an estimated 30,000 or more grizzly and brown bears. There are only about 1,000 bears in the northern United States where they are considered a threatened species. Brown bears live around the world in the very northern latitudes. Bears are popular attractions in zoos and wildlife parks, often placed there after being rescued as orphans in the wild. Bears generally live solitary lives and range over a home territory from 100 square miles to 500 square miles, depending on the animal's age and the food available.

Size and shape
Brown bears are distinguished from black bears by a hump at the shoulders, longer claws and shorter faces. They vary in color from light blond to dark brown with some cinnamon, blue-gray or blue-black colorings. Adult grizzly bears weigh between 200 to 900 pounds and can be up to nine feet long, with an occasional male weighing more than 1,500 pounds. Bears weigh the most just before retiring into their dens for the winter. Females weigh 1/2 to 3/4 as much as males.

Life span
Bears live 15 to 30 years in the wild but longer in captivity. They get some gray in the "muzzle" area as they age.

Tracks and signs
Each foot has five toes, each with non-retractable claws adapted for digging. Bears have a big toe on the outside of each foot; a front paw can range from 3-3/4" to 10" wide. Native tribes called bears "the beasts that walk like people." Other bear signs are digs, dens, rubbing trees, droppings, trails, and food sites. Bears often rub their flanks or back on trees.

Danger
Bear country is wild country. Bears are unpredictable and dangerous, with excellent hearing and sense of smell. Never run from a bear—their instinct is to chase. Make noises to let them know you are around; they will often run away. If confronted, back away slowly while talking to them and waving your arms to make yourself bigger. Never feed bears or leave food around your campsite. Burn or pack out all your garbage.

Joy Martin (1922-2012)

According to Joy, becoming a mother, mother-in-law and grandmother blessed her more than her formal educational degrees and teaching work. Throughout her lifetime, she wrote newspaper columns, children's literature and family-oriented stories. Joy also owned a nursery school for many years where she implemented many innovative ideas that she eventually showcased in her first book, Early To Learn (Dodd Mead, N.Y.).

Shannon Cartwright

Shannon Cartwright received her BFA degree from the University of Michigan in 1971 and expresses her love for Alaska through her illustrations, sculptures and jewelry.

She has lived in Alaska since 1972 and has illustrated or written more than 25 children's books including *Alaska Animals You and I*, *Bear Story*, *Train Story*, *Ol'556* and *Alaska's Three Bears*. She lives "off the grid" in a remote cabin along the Alaska Railroad where her every day close-to-nature experiences inspire her creations.

Note to readers...

This book includes text set in both printed and cursive (handwritten) forms to help teach reading and writing skills to children of all ages. Many of the illustrations in this book include a secret animal or plant that keys to the main letter. For example, there is a nuthatch in the letter N artwork and kinglet in the letter K artwork. See how many others you can find!

Vist GreatlandGraphics.com to purchase more of Shannon's popular children's books including *Alaska Animals You and I*, and her board books: *Alaska Numbers 123*, *Alaska's ABC Bears*, *Alaska's Train Story*.

GREATLAND GRAPHICS
3875 Geist Rd, Ste E PMB 449
Fairbanks, Alaska 99709
(907) 337-1234
GreatlandGraphics.com